LIMITarchitects (Ed.)

T0334950

shape

Is global design generic?

From form to meaning, fantasy to reality

Juhani Pallasmaa, architect, professor (Helsinki)

Over the past three decades, we have been witnessing an unforeseen era of architectural euphoria. New technologies and production methods, computerized and computational design processes, commercial competition, and fluid globalized capital have made any conceivable form and structure technically feasible. Indeed, architectural journals are repeatedly presenting projects that border on the possible and believable. This deliberate artificiality and distance from the human reality of things has become the accepted measure of quality.

In den letzten drei Jahrzehnten haben wir ein Zeitalter unvorhergesehener Euphorie in der Architektur erlebt. Durch die neuen Technologien und Produktionsmethoden, die rechnergestützten Designprozesse, den kommerzorientierten Wettbewerb und die globalisierten Kapitalströmungen ist jede Form und jede Struktur technisch möglich geworden. In Architekturzeitschriften werden immer wieder Projekte vorgestellt, in denen die Grenzen des Möglichen und Glaubhaften immer weiter verschoben werden. Diese bewusste Künstlichkeit und diese Entfernung von der menschlichen Realität sind zu einem üblichen Maßstab für Qualität geworden.

Nous assistons depuis trente ans à une ère inattendue d'euphorie architecturale. Les nouvelles technologies et méthodes de production, l'informatisation de la conception, la concurrence commerciale et les flux globaux de capital ont rendu réalisable chaque forme ou structure imaginable. En effet, les magazines d'architecture présentent invariablement des projets à la frontière du possible ou du crédible. Ce parti pris de l'artificiel et de l'éloignement d'une réalité humaine est devenu un critère consensuel de qualité.

Yet - architectural meaning does not arise from curiosities or spatial fantasy, spectacular forms, or complex geometries. Meaning is grounded in human existential experience. Architecture is not essentially a formal game or play with abstraction; it is deeply involved in human memory and meaning. True architecture does not display formal ingenuity, as it articulates our very experiences of being and gives meaning and dignity to our sense of the world and ourselves. Profound architectural experiences arise from our encounter with existentially meaningful places, spaces and situations that mediate our relationships with the world, time and the course of culture. Sensible buildings enable us to grasp the continuum of time and culture, and they structure and articulate our experiences of being. Profound architecture is more about human fate, dignity and potential than formal fabrication.

Bedeutung in der Architektur entspringt aber nicht Sonderbarkeiten oder der räumlichen Fantasie, spektakulären oder komplexen geometrischen Formen, sondern gründet vielmehr auf die menschliche Erfahrung des Existenziellen. Ihrem Wesen nach ist Architektur ebenso wenig ein formelles Spiel mit Abstraktem, denn sie liegt dem menschlichen Gedächtnis und der Suche nach Bedeutung zugrunde. Wahre Architektur zeugt nicht von formeller Genialität, sondern verleiht als Ausdruck unserer existentiellen Grunderfahrungen unserem Weltempfinden und unserer Selbstwahrnehmung Bedeutung und Würde. Intensive Erfahrungen vermittels Architektur entstehen aus unserer Begegnung mit existentiell bedeutsamen Orten, Räumen und Situationen, die unsere Beziehung zur Welt, Zeit und Kultur vermitteln. Sinnvolle Gebäude machen es uns erst möglich, das Kontinuum von Zeit und Kultur zu erfassen und geben unseren existentiellen Erfahrungen Struktur und Ausdruck. Ernste Architektur hat mehr mit dem menschlichen Schicksal, Würde und Potential zu tun als mit formeller Fabrikation.

Or, le sens en architecture ne résulte pas de curiosités, d'imagination spatiale, de formes spectaculaires ou de géométries complexes. Le sens repose sur l'expérience humaine de l'existence. L'architecture n'est pas fondamentalement un jeu formel avec l'abstraction ; elle est profondément ancrée dans la mémoire et la logique humaines. La véritable architecture n'affiche pas d'ingénuité formelle, elle exprime notre rapport même à l'existence et donne du poids et du sens à notre perception du monde et de nous-même. La profonde expérience de l'architecture naît de notre rencontre avec des endroits, des espaces et des situations porteurs de sens existentiel et qui interviennent dans notre relation avec le monde, le temps et la culture. Les bâtiments fonctionnels nous permettent de saisir la trajectoire du temps et de la culture, ils structurent et traduisent notre expérience de l'être. L'architecture profonde touche davantage au sort, à la dignité et au potentiel humains qu'à la création formelle.

In today's realm of art, it is commonly believed that artistic quality arises from the uniqueness and self-expression of the artist. Yet, Balthus, one of the greatest figurative painters of last century, presents an opposite view: 'If a work only expresses the person who created it, it wasn't worth doing... Expressing the world, understanding it, that is what seems interesting to me'. All great works of art express the conditions of our own being-in-the-world through the unique sensitivity and empathic capacity of the individual artist. It is the empathic subtlety of the artist that invites us to enter the specific universe of the work, not its intellectual wit or formal inventiveness. As Jean-Paul Sartre suggests, 'If the painter presents us with a field or a vase of flowers, his paintings are windows which are open to the whole world'.

In der heutigen Kunstwelt glaubt man allgemein, dass künstlerische Qualität ein Ergebnis der künstlerischen Einzigartigkeit und des Selbstausdrucks ist. Balthus, einer der größten figurativen Maler des letzten Jahrhunderts, hielt jedoch eine entgegengesetzte Sicht: „Wenn das Werk nur den Menschen, der es schuf zum Ausdruck bringt, dann war es überhaupt nicht wert, es zu machen... Der Welt Ausdruck verleihen, die Welt verstehen, das ist was mir interessant erscheint." Alle großen Kunstwerke sind aufgrund der einzigartigen Empfindsamkeit und der Empathie des einzelnen Künstlers Ausdruck der Bedingungen unseres In-der-Welt-Seins. Es ist die empathische Subtilität des Künstlers, die uns dazu auffordert, in das spezifische Universum des Werkes einzutreten, und nicht der intellektuelle Witz oder der formelle Erfindungsreichtum. Wie Jean-Paul Sartre einmal sagte: „Wenn der Maler uns ein Feld oder eine Blumenvase vorsetzt, dann sind seine Bilder Fenster, die sich zur ganzen Welt hin öffnen."

Aujourd'hui, dans le domaine des arts, il est généralement admis que la qualité artistique est le produit de l'originalité et de l'expression personnelle de l'artiste. Pourtant, Balthus, l'un des plus grands peintres figuratifs du siècle dernier, est d'un autre avis : « si une œuvre exprime seulement la personne qui l'a créée, alors elle n'en vaut pas la peine... Exprimer le monde, le comprendre, c'est cela qui me semble intéressant ». Toutes les grandes œuvres d'art expriment les circonstances de notre présence dans le monde à travers la sensibilité unique et la faculté empathique de l'artiste en tant qu'individu. Ce n'est pas l'intellect ou l'inventivité formelle de l'artiste, mais sa subtilité empathique qui nous invite à pénétrer l'univers particulier de son œuvre. Comme le dit Jean-Paul Sartre, « si le peintre nous présente un champ ou un vase de fleurs, ses tableaux sont des fenêtres ouvertes sur le monde entier. »

Today's architectural ambition is most often to create something that is unique and unforeseen. But in the world of art only things that evoke deep recollections and embodied memories can have meaning. Artistic meaning is born of resonance and recognition, not of alienation or the shock of the new. Instead of leading us into a fantasy world, the task of architecture is to strengthen and sensitize our understanding of the real. Especially in a time of surreal consumerism when everything in life turns increasingly fictitious, unreal and dream-like, it is the duty of art to re-energize and sharpen our relationship with reality. What art and architecture need most today is a combined sense of human reality, existential imagination and creative humility.

In der heutigen Architektur ist man meistens bestrebt, etwas Einzigartiges und Unvorhergesehenes zu schaffen. Doch in der Welt der Kunst können nur Dinge, die tiefe, konkrete Erinnerungen wachrufen, Bedeutung haben. Künstlerische Bedeutung entsteht aus Resonanz und Anerkennung, nicht aus Entfremdung oder aus der Schockwirkung des Neuen. Vor allem in unserer Zeit des surrealen Konsumdenkens, wenn alles im Leben zunehmend fiktiven, irrealen und traumartigen Charakter hat, ist es Aufgabe der Kunst, unsere Beziehung zur Realität neu zu beleben und zu schärfen. Was die Kunst und die Architektur beide heute am dringendsten benötigen, ist ein gemeinsamer Sinn für die menschliche Wirklichkeit, die existentielle Fantasie und die Demut vor dem kreativen Prozess.

L'ambition de l'architecture d'aujourd'hui est la plupart du temps de créer de l'unique et de l'imprévu. Mais en art, seuls les objets touchant à la mémoire profonde et à des souvenirs enracinés peuvent avoir un sens. Le sens artistique est le fruit de résonances et de reconnaissances, et non d'aliénations ou du choc de la nouveauté. Le rôle de l'architecture n'est pas de nous emmener dans un monde imaginaire, mais de renforcer et d'affiner notre compréhension du monde. A l'ère du consumérisme débridé, où tout dans nos vies est de plus en plus fictif, irréel et onirique, il est particulièrement du devoir de l'art de revitaliser et d'aiguiser notre rapport à la réalité. L'art et l'architecture ont aujourd'hui avant tout besoin d'une notion de la réalité humaine, d'imagination existentielle et d'humilité dans la création.

CHANEL MASCARA

DESIGN GABRIELLE BONHEUR CHANEL 2013
BY CHANEL
A TRIBUTE TO JEAN NOUVEL

TYPE V FORGED WHEEL

DESIGN MICHELE VIANDANTE 2013
BY SCHNITZER
A TRIBUTE TO PIER LUIGI NERVI

BEOCENTER 9000

DESIGN BANG AND OLUFSEN 1990
BY BANG AND OLUFSEN

ALVAR AALTO VASE

DESIGN ALVAR AALTO / PENTAGON DESIGN 1936
BY IITALA
A TRIBUTE TO SANAA

SKYLINE HOME THEATER SYSTEM

DESIGN CLAESSON KOIVISTO RUNE 2013
BY DAVID CARLSON

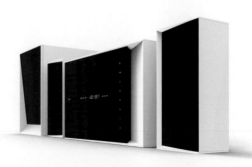

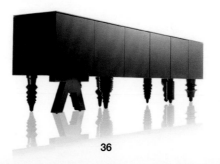

36

DYSON FAN HEATER

DESIGN JAMES DYSON 2010
BY DYSON

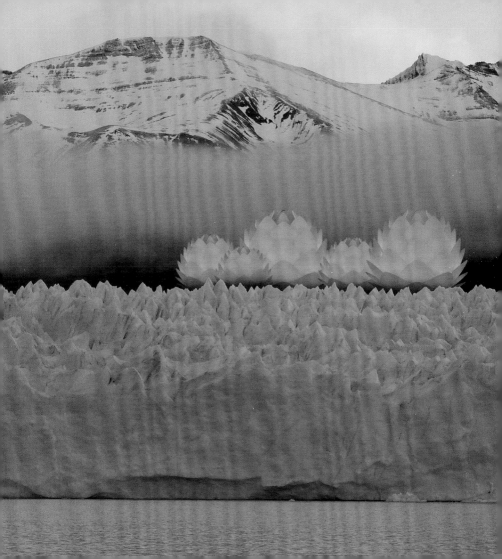

44

SERPENTINE BOTTLE OPENER

DESIGN TOM KOVAC 2008
BY ALESSI
A TRIBUTE TO ZAHA HADID

RIMOWA TOPAS MULTIWHEEL

DESIGN RIMOWA 1950 / 2013
BY RIMOWA

APPLE G5

DESIGN JONATHAN IVE & APPLE DESIGN TEAM 2003
BY APPLE

LUNA ROSSA

DESIGN YVES BEHAR / DANIELA ANDRIER 2012
BY PRADA
A TRIBUTE TO HANS HOLLEIN

LE SOLEIL PENDANT LIGHT

DESIGN VICENTE GARCIA JIMENEZ 2009
BY FOSCARINI
A TRIBUTE TO FRANK LLOYD WRIGHT

PANOS INFINITY LF LED DOWNLIGHT

DESIGN CHRIS REDFERN 2010
BY ZUMTOBEL

COPPER PENCIL HOLDER

DESIGN TRINE ANDERSEN 2012
BY FERM LIVING
A TRIBUTE TO LOUIS I. KAHN

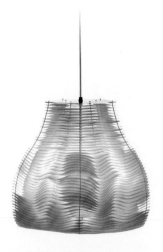

SOUNDBAR HTS8140

DESIGN PHILIPS 2009
BY PHILIPS

DESIGN VEHO 2014
BY VEHO

LACIE PORSCHE DESKTOP DRIVE

DESIGN PORSCHE 2011
BY LACIE

KISAI DENSHOKU LED WATCH

DESIGN TOKYOFLASH 2008
BY TOKYOFLASH

120

OSKAR BIG HUMIDIFIER

DESIGN STADLER FORM 2012
BY STADLER FORM

C3 TABLE

DESIGN SEBASTIAN DESCH 2010
BY TEAM 7
A TRIBUTE TO LUDWIG MIES VAN DER ROHE

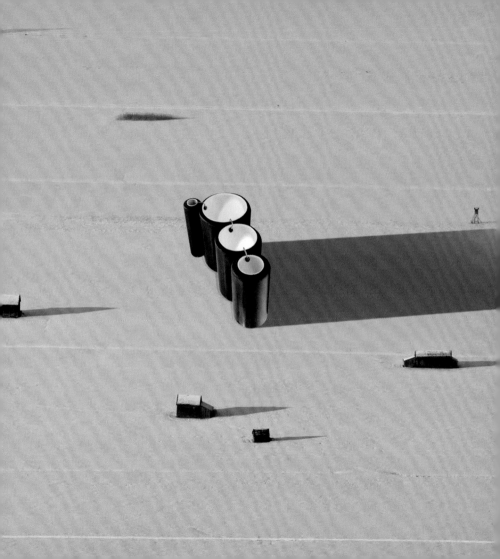

QLOCKTWO

DESIGN MARCO BIEGERT, ANDREAS FUNK 2009
BY BIEGERT & FUNK

T IS

ALF

AST

TWELVE

• • •

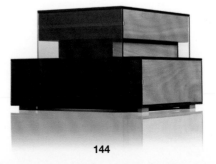

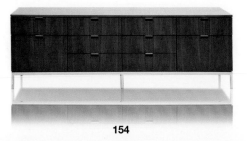

156

TUPPERWARE SPACEMAKER

DESIGN TUPPERWARE 2004
BY TUPPERWARE
A TRIBUTE TO KISHO KUROKAWA

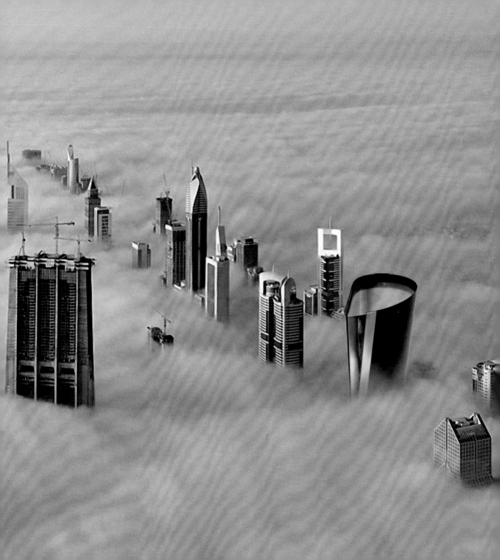

174

CONSOLE KASIMIR N°367

DESIGN HERVE VAN DER STRAETEN 2010
BY RALPH PUCCI
A TRIBUTE TO REM KOOLHAAS

GLASS BOOKSHELF

DESIGN GERALD LA STARZA 2012
BY BROOKLYNMODERN

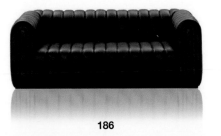

TOMATO CHAIR

DESIGN EERO AARNIO 1971
BY ASKO LAHTI

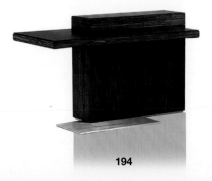

APPLE MACBOOK AIR 11 INCH

DESIGN JONATHAN IVE & APPLE DESIGN TEAM 2010
BY APPLE

O-SPACE

DESIGN LUCA NICHETTO UND GIANPIETRO GAI 2003
BY FOSCARINI
A TRIBUTE TO FUTURE SYSTEMS

APPLE IPHONE 5

DESIGN JONATHAN IVE & APPLE DESIGN TEAM 2012
BY APPLE

REK BOOKCASE

DESIGN REINIER DE JONG 2014
BY REINIER DE JONG DESIGN
A TRIBUTE TO PETER EISENMAN

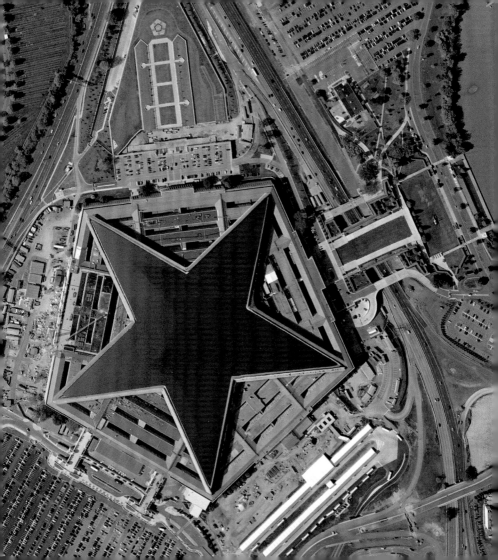

MONSANTO

AGRICULTURAL BIOTECHNOLOGY CORPORATION
FOUNDED IN 1901 IN ST. LOUIS, MISSOURI / USA

MONSANTO

LUFTHANSA

AIRLINE
FOUNDED IN 1926/1953 IN KÖLN / GERMANY

MC DONALDS
FAST FOOD RESTAURANT
FOUNDED IN 1940 IN SAN BERNARDINO, CALIFORNIA / USA

SAMSUNG

MULTINATIONAL CONGLOMERATE COMPANY
FOUNDED IN 1938 IN DAEGU / SOUTH KOREA

MoMA

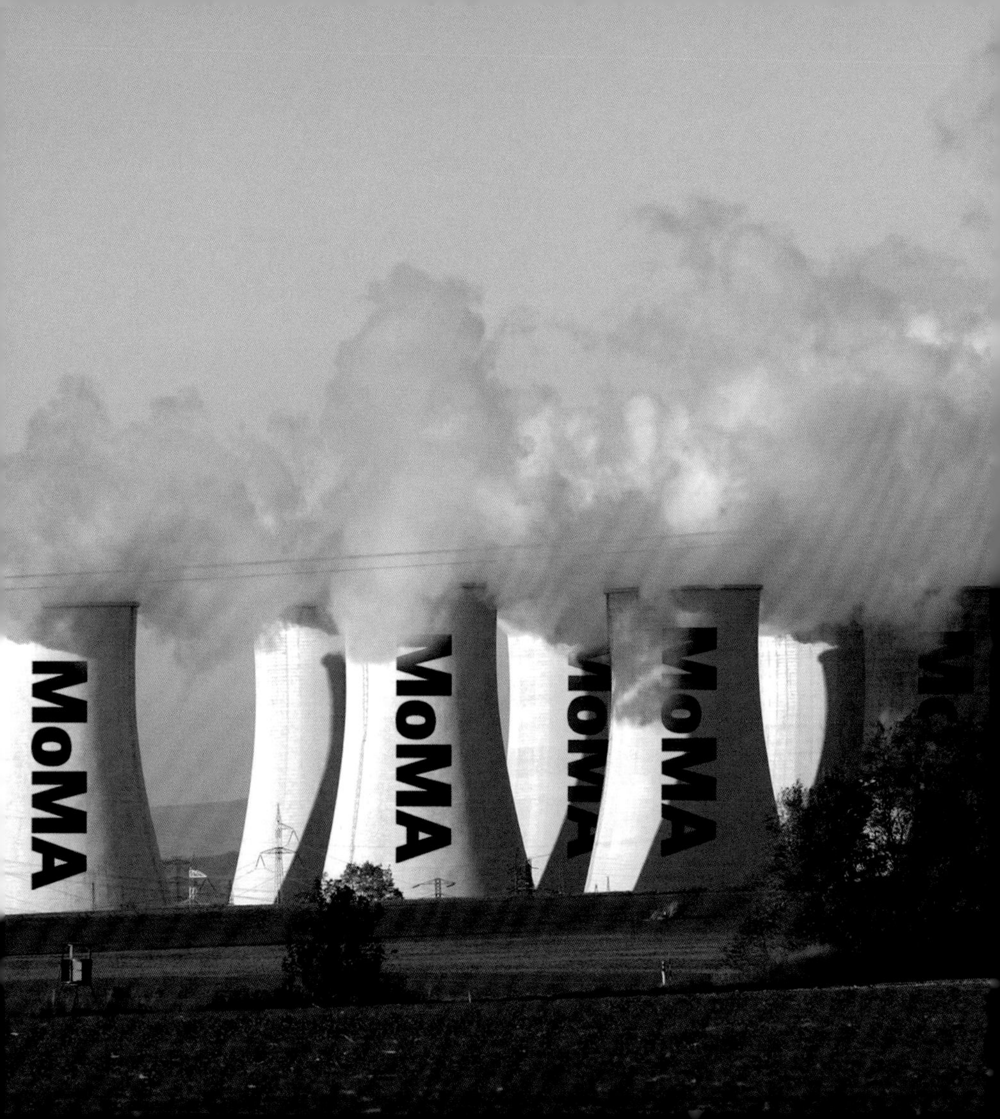
MoMA
MoMA
MoMA
MoMA

WALMART

RETAIL CORPORATION
FOUNDED IN 1962 IN ROGERS, ARKANSAS / USA

Wolfgang Bürgler

Wolfgang Bürgler, born in 1961 in Radstadt/Austria studied at the University of Applied Arts, Vienna. He was a co-founder of the firm 'the office' in 1991 and 'the unit' in 1996, both based in Vienna. In 2003 he established the firm 'LIMIT architects' in Vienna that he also heads. LIMIT architects has received several national and international awards.

Richard Oberriedmüller

Richard Oberriedmüller, born in 1971 in Vienna/Austria. Graphic designer and art director in several design and advertising agencies. Self-employed designer since 1999. Intensive teamwork with architectural offices and elaboration of structural projects, high affinity to architectural projects and shop design. Awards for his graphic arts and environmental designs.

Juhani Pallasmaa

Juhani Pallasmaa (b. 1936), architect, professor emeritus, Helsinki. He first practiced design in collaboration with other architects, and in 1983-2012 through his own office in Helsinki. He has held numerous positions, such as Rector of the Institute of Industrial Design, Director of the Museum of Finnish Architecture and Professor and Dean of the School of Architecture, Helsinki University of Technology. He has had several visiting professorships in the USA and taught and lectured in a variety of universities in Europe, North and South America, Africa, Asia and Australia. Pallasmaa has published 45 books and 350 essays, and his writings have been translated into over thirty languages. He is honorary member of SAFA, AIA and RIBA, Academician of the International Academy of Architecture, and has received several Finnish and international awards and five Honorary Doctorates.

Credits

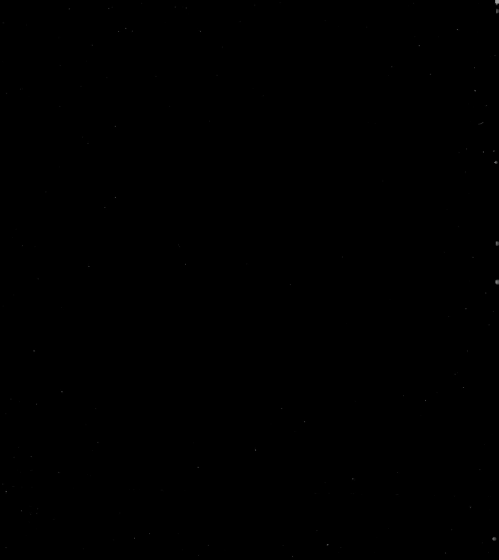

Imprint

Editor, Idea and Conception
LIMITarchitects / Wolfgang Bürgler / www.limit.at

Preface
Juhani Pallasmaa

Graphic Design, Renderings
Richard Oberriedmüller / www.oberriedmueller.at

Coordination
Sascha Niemann

Transalation
Camilla Nielsen (en) and Valentine Elleau (fr)

Photocredits Research
Günter Göbhart and Eric Moser

Publisher
© 2014 AMBRA | V
AMBRA | V is part of Medecco Holding GmbH, Vienna
Printed in Austria

Production
0816 Printproduktion GmbH, Vienna / www.nullacht16.at

Printed by
Paul Gerin GmbH & Co KG, Wolkersdorf / www.gerin.co.at

ISBN 978-3-99043-670-7